JOURNAL

BY THE EDITORS OF

Prevention.

RODALE.

© 2017 by Rodale Inc.

Rodale books may be purchased for business or promotional use or for special sales. For information, please write to:
Special Markets Department, Rodale, Inc., 733 Third Avenue, New York, NY 10017

Prevention is a registered trademark of Rodale Inc.

Printed in China

Rodale Inc. makes every effort to use acid-free ♾, recycled paper ♻.

Background pattern (page 8) © Vera Petruk/Getty Images
Watercolor wash (page 10) © Juan Facundo Mora Soria/Getty Images
Face icons (page 11) © popcic/Getty Images
Water glass (page 11) © Rakdee/Getty Images

Book design by Carol Angstadt

ISBN 978–1–62336–911–8 direct paperback

2 4 6 8 10 9 7 5 3   paperback

We inspire health, healing, happiness, and love in the world. Starting with you.

"Each morning
we are born again.
What we do today is
what matters most."

—BUDDHA

Your Transformation Starts Here

GET MOTIVATED AND TRACK YOUR PROGRESS

Before you get started, take 10 minutes to remind yourself why you've decided to put your health and fitness first. You'll be able to refer back to these goals at any time during your weight loss journey to remind yourself of the big picture and stay motivated.

At the end of this program, I . . .

... WANT TO FEEL _____

_____

... WANT TO LOOK _____

_____

... WANT TO BE ABLE TO EXPERIENCE _____

_____

Personal Stats

If you're a numbers person, now is a good time to record your weight
and measurements so you can monitor your progress. Remember, the
scale can't tell you how much you're loved or how awesome you are—it's
only a number, but it does factor into our health. So record it, let it go,
and remember you are moving toward a healthier lifestyle starting
today. The Weight Loss Tracker on the next page is set up for weighing
once per cycle or every day. Your choice.

	STARTING	ENDING		STARTING	ENDING
WEIGHT			R UPPER ARM		
PANTS SIZE			L UPPER ARM		
DRESS SIZE			R THIGH		
BRA SIZE			L THIGH		
CHEST			R CALF		
WAIST			L CALF		
HIPS			NECK		

✳ Use a tape measure to measure at the widest point of each body part.

Weight Loss Tracker

Weigh yourself at the end of each cycle or
every day, whatever method works best for you.

	DAY	DATE	WEIGHT	LOSS		DAY	DATE	WEIGHT	LOSS
CYCLE 1	1				**CYCLE 4**	31			
	2					32			
	3					33			
	4					34			
	5					35			
	6					36			
	7					37			
	8					38			
	9					39			
	10					40			
CYCLE 2	11				**CYCLE 5**	41			
	12					42			
	13					43			
	14					44			
	15					45			
	16					46			
	17					47			
	18					48			
	19					49			
	20					50			
CYCLE 3	21				**CYCLE 6**	51			
	22					52			
	23					53			
	24					54			
	25					55			
	26					56			
	27					57			
	28					58			
	29					59			
	30					60			

Create Your Motivational Mantra

The way we talk to ourselves matters. Take a moment to come up with your own personal mantra. This is a repetitive word or sentence that will give you strength and motivation during those moments when you want to skip a workout or eat something that won't make you feel great in the long run. Remember: You are worth it! Here are some examples of mantras. Try one of these or create your own.

Strong today, stronger tomorrow.

What I feed my body, I feed my soul.

My thoughts create my feelings;
my feelings create my actions.

I can move toward my goals or away from them.

My body is strong. My body is beautiful.
I will treat it well.

My Mantra

_____

_____

_____

_____

Snap a "Before" Pic on Day 1.

This is your starting point–use it to track
your progress on the program!

{ **DATE:** }

Snap an "After" Pic on Day 60.

You've completed the program—congrats! Compare this with your "Before" picture to see how far you've come.

{ DATE: }

{ **DATE:**
2/16/17 }

*"Success is the sum of small efforts,
repeated day in and day out!"*

—ROBERT J. COLLIER

1☺-MINUTE LIFE CHANGERS

Squeeze in these mini but mighty challenges to speed your results and feel great.

SET YOURSELF UP FOR SUCCESS : Write down your three biggest goals for today.

1 *Prepare my meals for the week*

2 *Stretch for 10 minutes after workout*

3 *Drink one more glass of water than yesterday*

10-MINUTE RECHARGE

What *Meditated in bed before I started my day.* ⏱ *7:00 am*

10-MINUTE MINDFUL MEAL

What *Lunch* ⏱ *12:30 pm*

10-MINUTE WALK

Where *Took the dog for a walk in the park.* ⏱ *6:15 pm*

10-MINUTE TECH BREAK

What *Unplugged and read a book with my kids.* ⏱ *8:30 pm*

NOTES: *I accomplished all of my goals for the day!*

fit in 🕙 TONING TRACKER _____ ☑ Yes, I did my Fit in 10 workout!

TODAY'S WORKOUT: Ultimate Booty Lifter

WORKOUT NOTES: How did you feel today? What progress are you making when it comes to your strength and fitness goals? Jot it down here.

Today I increased my hand weights to 8 lbs! I'm feeling

stronger with each cycle.

fit in 🕙 FOOD TRACKER _____

BREAKFAST: *Soft-Boiled Egg with Sweet Potato Toast Soldiers*

SNACK: *Pear Wrapped in Cheddar and Prosciutto*

LUNCH: *Chicken and Bacon Pizza*

DINNER: *Speedy Fish Tacos*

SNACK: *Banana Peanut Butter "Ice Cream" Parfait*

fit in 🕙 WATER TRACKER _____

Aim to drink ten 8-ounce glasses of H_2O each day. Cross them off as you go!

fit in 🕙 MOOD TRACKER _____

How are you feeling today? Circle any that apply and make notes below.

HAPPY PROUD FOCUSED ENERGIZED STRONG SAD TIRED FRUSTRATED

NOTES: *I'm proud of myself for accomplishing my three goals, and I'm feeling strong after using heavier weights in my workout.*

Cycle
1

DAYS 1–10

*"Go confidently in the direction
of your dreams.
Live the life you have imagined."*

—HENRY DAVID THOREAU

Welcome to your first cycle on the Fit in 10 Plan. Now's your chance to clean up your diet and kick-start your workouts. With every cycle, we'll be adding a 10-Minute Life Changer to improve your day, just 10 minutes at a time. Be sure to jot down all of your meals and snacks in the allotted space—it's one of the easiest ways to reach your goals!

1Ⓞ-MINUTE LIFE CHANGER
Set Yourself Up for Success

It's time to get focused. Research shows that people who plan their days are more likely to accomplish their top priorities. Women and men who write down their goals complete significantly more over a 4-week span than those who don't write any aspirations at all, according to a study from Dominican University of California. What's more, those who share their commitment and weekly progress reports with a friend achieve even greater success than those who only put them down on paper.

Take 10 minutes each morning to jot down your top three goals for the day, and try to do them early, when your willpower is still strong. These items should help you move closer toward your long-term goals of being stronger, healthier, and happier. Then share your daily, weekly, and monthly intentions with your partner or a friend, or even via your social network.

{ DATE: }

"Nothing is impossible, the word itself says, 'I'm possible!'"

—AUDREY HEPBURN

1Ⓞ-MINUTE LIFE CHANGERS

Squeeze in these mini but mighty challenges to speed your results and feel great.

SET YOURSELF UP FOR SUCCESS: Write down your three biggest goals for today.

1 _____

2 _____

3 _____

NOTES: _____

_____

_____

_____

_____

_____

_____

_____

_____

_____

_____

_____

fit IN 10 TONING TRACKER

TODAY'S WORKOUT: Lean and Lovely Legs

WORKOUT NOTES: How did you feel today? What progress are you making when it comes to your strength and fitness goals? Jot it down here.

_____

_____

fit IN 10 FOOD TRACKER

BREAKFAST: _____

SNACK: _____

LUNCH: _____

DINNER: _____

SNACK: _____

fit IN 10 WATER TRACKER

Aim to drink ten 8-ounce glasses of H_2O each day. Cross them off as you go!

🥛 🥛 🥛 🥛 🥛 🥛 🥛 🥛 🥛 🥛

fit IN 10 MOOD TRACKER

How are you feeling today? Circle any that apply and make notes below.

😄	🙂	🤓	😵	😁	🙁	😮	😫
HAPPY	**PROUD**	**FOCUSED**	**ENERGIZED**	**STRONG**	**SAD**	**TIRED**	**FRUSTRATED**

NOTES: _____

_____

_____

{ DATE: }

"The most effective way to do it, is to do it."

—AMELIA EARHART

10-MINUTE LIFE CHANGERS

Squeeze in these mini but mighty challenges to speed your results and feel great.

SET YOURSELF UP FOR SUCCESS: Write down your three biggest goals for today.

1 _____

2 _____

3 _____

NOTES: _____

_____

_____

_____

_____

_____

_____

_____

_____

_____

_____

fit in 10 TONING TRACKER

☐ Yes, I did my Fit in 10 workout!

TODAY'S WORKOUT: Back to Strong

WORKOUT NOTES: How did you feel today? What progress are you making when it comes to your strength and fitness goals? Jot it down here.

_____

_____

fit in 10 FOOD TRACKER

BREAKFAST: _____

SNACK: _____

LUNCH: _____

DINNER: _____

SNACK: _____

fit in 10 WATER TRACKER

Aim to drink ten 8-ounce glasses of H_2O each day. Cross them off as you go!

fit in 10 MOOD TRACKER

How are you feeling today? Circle any that apply and make notes below.

HAPPY	PROUD	FOCUSED	ENERGIZED	STRONG	SAD	TIRED	FRUSTRATED

NOTES: _____

_____

_____

{ DATE: }

"At the end of the day, tell yourself gently: 'I love you, you did the best you could today, and even if you didn't accomplish all you had planned, I love you anyway.'"

—FRANÇOIS

⏱-MINUTE LIFE CHANGERS

Squeeze in these mini but mighty challenges to speed your results and feel great.

SET YOURSELF UP FOR SUCCESS: Write down your three biggest goals for today.

1 _____

2 _____

3 _____

NOTES: _____

_____

_____

_____

_____

_____

_____

_____

_____

_____

_____

fit in 10 TONING TRACKER

☐ Yes, I did my Fit in 10 workout!

TODAY'S WORKOUT: Deep Core

WORKOUT NOTES: How did you feel today? What progress are you making when it comes to your strength and fitness goals? Jot it down here.

_____

_____

fit in 10 FOOD TRACKER

BREAKFAST: _____

SNACK: _____

LUNCH: _____

DINNER: _____

SNACK: _____

fit in 10 WATER TRACKER

Aim to drink ten 8-ounce glasses of H_2O each day. Cross them off as you go!

fit in 10 MOOD TRACKER

How are you feeling today? Circle any that apply and make notes below.

HAPPY   PROUD   FOCUSED   ENERGIZED   STRONG   SAD   TIRED   FRUSTRATED

NOTES: _____

_____

_____

{ DATE: }

*"What would you attempt to do
if you knew you could not fail?"*

—UNKNOWN

──────── **1⊘-MINUTE LIFE CHANGERS** ────────

Squeeze in these mini but mighty challenges to speed your results and feel great.

SET YOURSELF UP FOR SUCCESS: Write down your three biggest goals for today.

1 _____

2 _____

3 _____

NOTES: _____

_____

_____

_____

_____

_____

_____

_____

_____

_____

_____

fit in 10 TONING TRACKER

☐ Yes, I did my Fit in 10 workout!

TODAY'S WORKOUT: Happy Hipster

WORKOUT NOTES: How did you feel today? What progress are you making when it comes to your strength and fitness goals? Jot it down here.

_____

_____

fit in 10 FOOD TRACKER

BREAKFAST: _____

SNACK: _____

LUNCH: _____

DINNER: _____

SNACK: _____

fit in 10 WATER TRACKER

Aim to drink ten 8-ounce glasses of H_2O each day. Cross them off as you go!

fit in 10 MOOD TRACKER

How are you feeling today? Circle any that apply and make notes below.

| HAPPY | PROUD | FOCUSED | ENERGIZED | STRONG | SAD | TIRED | FRUSTRATED |

NOTES: _____

_____

"Always be a first-rate version of yourself, instead of a second-rate version of somebody else."

—JUDY GARLAND

10-MINUTE LIFE CHANGERS

Squeeze in these mini but mighty challenges to speed your results and feel great.

SET YOURSELF UP FOR SUCCESS: Write down your three biggest goals for today.

1 _____

2 _____

3 _____

NOTES: _____

_____

_____

_____

_____

_____

_____

_____

_____

_____

_____

fit in 10 TONING TRACKER

☐ Yes, I did my Fit in 10 workout!

TODAY'S WORKOUT: Dare to Bare Arms

WORKOUT NOTES: How did you feel today? What progress are you making when it comes to your strength and fitness goals? Jot it down here.

_____

_____

fit in 10 FOOD TRACKER

BREAKFAST: _____

SNACK: _____

LUNCH: _____

DINNER: _____

SNACK: _____

fit in 10 WATER TRACKER

Aim to drink ten 8-ounce glasses of H_2O each day. Cross them off as you go!

fit in 10 MOOD TRACKER

How are you feeling today? Circle any that apply and make notes below.

HAPPY   PROUD   FOCUSED   ENERGIZED   STRONG   SAD   TIRED   FRUSTRATED

NOTES: _____

_____

_____

{ DATE: }

"You can't fall if you don't climb. But there's no joy in living your whole life on the ground."

—UNKNOWN

1⦿-MINUTE LIFE CHANGERS

Squeeze in these mini but mighty challenges to speed your results and feel great.

SET YOURSELF UP FOR SUCCESS : Write down your three biggest goals for today.

1 _____

2 _____

3 _____

NOTES: _____

_____

_____

_____

_____

_____

_____

_____

_____

_____

_____

fit IN **10** TONING TRACKER _____ ☐ Yes, I did my Fit in 10 workout!

TODAY'S WORKOUT: Flat and Firm Abs

WORKOUT NOTES: How did you feel today? What progress are you making when it comes to your strength and fitness goals? Jot it down here.

_____

_____

fit IN **10** FOOD TRACKER _____

BREAKFAST: _____

SNACK: _____

LUNCH: _____

DINNER: _____

SNACK: _____

fit IN **10** WATER TRACKER _____

Aim to drink ten 8-ounce glasses of H_2O each day. Cross them off as you go!

fit IN **10** MOOD TRACKER _____

How are you feeling today? Circle any that apply and make notes below.

HAPPY   PROUD   FOCUSED   ENERGIZED   STRONG   SAD   TIRED   FRUSTRATED

NOTES: _____

_____

_____

{ DATE: }

"Take time to deliberate; but when the time for action arrives, stop thinking and go in."

—ANDREW JACKSON

10-MINUTE LIFE CHANGERS

Squeeze in these mini but mighty challenges to speed your results and feel great.

SET YOURSELF UP FOR SUCCESS: Write down your three biggest goals for today.

1 _____

2 _____

3 _____

NOTES: _____

_____

_____

_____

_____

_____

_____

_____

_____

_____

_____

fit ⏱ TONING TRACKER _____ ☐ Yes, I did my Fit in 10 workout!

TODAY'S WORKOUT: Ultimate Booty Lifter

WORKOUT NOTES: How did you feel today? What progress are you making when it comes to your strength and fitness goals? Jot it down here.

_____

_____

fit ⏱ FOOD TRACKER _____

BREAKFAST: _____

SNACK: _____

LUNCH: _____

DINNER: _____

SNACK: _____

fit ⏱ WATER TRACKER _____

Aim to drink ten 8-ounce glasses of H_2O each day. Cross them off as you go!

🥛 🥛 🥛 🥛 🥛 🥛 🥛 🥛 🥛 🥛

fit ⏱ MOOD TRACKER _____

How are you feeling today? Circle any that apply and make notes below.

😄 😊 🤓 😵 😁 🙁 😮 😫
HAPPY PROUD FOCUSED ENERGIZED STRONG SAD TIRED FRUSTRATED

NOTES: _____

_____

_____

{ DATE: }

"Success is dependent upon the glands—sweat glands."

—ZIG ZIGLAR

1⏱-MINUTE LIFE CHANGERS

Squeeze in these mini but mighty challenges to speed your results and feel great.

SET YOURSELF UP FOR SUCCESS: Write down your three biggest goals for today.

1 _____

2 _____

3 _____

NOTES: _____

_____

_____

_____

_____

_____

_____

_____

_____

_____

_____

fit IN 10 TONING TRACKER _____ ☐ Yes, I did my Fit in 10 workout!

TODAY'S WORKOUT: Totally Toned Triceps

WORKOUT NOTES: How did you feel today? What progress are you making when it comes to your strength and fitness goals? Jot it down here.

_____

_____

fit IN 10 FOOD TRACKER _____

BREAKFAST: _____

SNACK: _____

LUNCH: _____

DINNER: _____

SNACK: _____

fit IN 10 WATER TRACKER _____

Aim to drink ten 8-ounce glasses of H_2O each day. Cross them off as you go!

fit IN 10 MOOD TRACKER _____

How are you feeling today? Circle any that apply and make notes below.

HAPPY   PROUD   FOCUSED   ENERGIZED   STRONG   SAD   TIRED   FRUSTRATED

NOTES: _____

_____

_____

DAY 9

*"I'm not afraid of the storms,
for I'm learning to sail my ship."*

—LOUISA MAY ALCOTT

1⏱-MINUTE LIFE CHANGERS

Squeeze in these mini but mighty challenges to speed your results and feel great.

SET YOURSELF UP FOR SUCCESS: Write down your three biggest goals for today.

1 _____

2 _____

3 _____

NOTES: _____

_____

_____

_____

_____

_____

_____

_____

_____

_____

_____

_____

fit IN 10 TONING TRACKER _____ ☐ Yes, I did my Fit in 10 workout!

TODAY'S WORKOUT: Lean and Lovely Legs

WORKOUT NOTES: How did you feel today? What progress are you making when it comes to your strength and fitness goals? Jot it down here.

_____

_____

fit IN 10 FOOD TRACKER _____

BREAKFAST: _____

SNACK: _____

LUNCH: _____

DINNER: _____

SNACK: _____

fit IN 10 WATER TRACKER _____

Aim to drink ten 8-ounce glasses of H_2O each day. Cross them off as you go!

🥛 🥛 🥛 🥛 🥛 🥛 🥛 🥛 🥛 🥛

fit IN 10 MOOD TRACKER _____

How are you feeling today? Circle any that apply and make notes below.

😄 HAPPY 🙂 PROUD 🤓 FOCUSED 😵 ENERGIZED 😊 STRONG 🙁 SAD 😮 TIRED 😣 FRUSTRATED

NOTES: _____

_____

_____

{ DATE: }

*"Energy and persistence
conquer all things."*

—BENJAMIN FRANKLIN

1⊙-MINUTE LIFE CHANGERS

Squeeze in these mini but mighty challenges to speed your results and feel great.

SET YOURSELF UP FOR SUCCESS: Write down your three biggest goals for today.

1 _____

2 _____

3 _____

NOTES: _____

_____

_____

_____

_____

_____

_____

_____

_____

_____

_____

fit IN 10 TONING TRACKER ____ ☐ Yes, I did my Fit in 10 workout!

TODAY'S WORKOUT: Meta Blast

WORKOUT NOTES: How did you feel today? What progress are you making when it comes to your strength and fitness goals? Jot it down here.

_____

_____

fit IN 10 FOOD TRACKER

BREAKFAST: _____

SNACK: _____

LUNCH: _____

DINNER: _____

SNACK: _____

fit IN 10 WATER TRACKER

Aim to drink ten 8-ounce glasses of H_2O each day. Cross them off as you go!

fit IN 10 MOOD TRACKER

How are you feeling today? Circle any that apply and make notes below.

HAPPY · PROUD · FOCUSED · ENERGIZED · STRONG · SAD · TIRED · FRUSTRATED

NOTES: _____

_____

_____

Cycle
2

DAYS 11–20

*"Put all excuses aside
and remember this:
YOU are capable."*

—ZIG ZIGLAR

Welcome to your second cycle of the Fit in 10 Plan. How are you feeling? Hopefully, you're starting to see what a difference simple clean eating and mini-but-mighty toning routines can make in your energy levels and body. Maybe you've even lost weight or you're starting to notice that your pants fit a little more loosely.

If you found the first cycle challenging, remember that making new habits takes time and it won't always be easy. Just stick with the plan and continue to focus on how amazing eating clean and moving a little more makes you feel.

On this new cycle, the Fit in 10 routines will become a little more challenging to keep your brain and body guessing and to speed results. Be sure to continue journaling your meals, as it's one of the easiest ways to ensure your success on the plan.

We'll also be adding another 10-Minute Life Changer to this cycle. Find your Life Changer below and commit to doing it each day.

10-MINUTE LIFE CHANGER
10-Minute Recharge

When you're super busy with work deadlines, family duties, and other social obligations, it's easy for the day to slip away without giving yourself a little TLC. This can open a window of unnecessary stress. Starting today, aim to schedule a daily 10-Minute Recharge for yourself. It can be anything you enjoy doing that gives you a chance to relax and reboot. Perhaps you read a magazine, enjoy your coffee, or take a walk. According to research at Harvard Medical School, 10 to 15 minutes of mindfulness a day is all you need for total mind-body relaxation. So use this time to take stock of the commitment you've made to getting healthy, and look forward to the wonderful new opportunities you are opening up for yourself.

{ DATE: }

"Success is not measured by what you accomplish but by the opposition you have encountered, and the courage with which you have maintained the struggle against overwhelming odds."

—ORISON SWETT MARDEN

10-MINUTE LIFE CHANGERS

Squeeze in these mini but mighty challenges to speed your results and feel great.

SET YOURSELF UP FOR SUCCESS: Write down your three biggest goals for today.

1 _____

2 _____

3 _____

10-MINUTE RECHARGE

What _____ 🕐 _____

NOTES: _____

_____

_____

_____

_____

_____

_____

fit in 10 TONING TRACKER

☐ Yes, I did my Fit in 10 workout!

TODAY'S WORKOUT: Tummy Love

WORKOUT NOTES: How did you feel today? What progress are you making when it comes to your strength and fitness goals? Jot it down here.

fit in 10 FOOD TRACKER

BREAKFAST:

SNACK:

LUNCH:

DINNER:

SNACK:

fit in 10 WATER TRACKER

Aim to drink ten 8-ounce glasses of H_2O each day. Cross them off as you go!

fit in 10 MOOD TRACKER

How are you feeling today? Circle any that apply and make notes below.

HAPPY   PROUD   FOCUSED   ENERGIZED   STRONG   SAD   TIRED   FRUSTRATED

NOTES:

{ DATE: }

"Love yourself first and everything else falls into line. You really have to love yourself to get anything done in this world."

—LUCILLE BALL

──── 10-MINUTE LIFE CHANGERS ────

Squeeze in these mini but mighty challenges to speed your results and feel great.

SET YOURSELF UP FOR SUCCESS : Write down your three biggest goals for today.

1 _____

2 _____

3 _____

10-MINUTE RECHARGE

What _____ 🕑 _____

NOTES: _____

_____

_____

_____

_____

_____

_____

fit in 10 TONING TRACKER

☐ Yes, I did my Fit in 10 workout!

TODAY'S WORKOUT: Ultimate Booty Lifter

WORKOUT NOTES: How did you feel today? What progress are you making when it comes to your strength and fitness goals? Jot it down here.

fit in 10 FOOD TRACKER

BREAKFAST:

SNACK:

LUNCH:

DINNER:

SNACK:

fit in 10 WATER TRACKER

Aim to drink ten 8-ounce glasses of H_2O each day. Cross them off as you go!

fit in 10 MOOD TRACKER

How are you feeling today? Circle any that apply and make notes below.

HAPPY   PROUD   FOCUSED   ENERGIZED   STRONG   SAD   TIRED   FRUSTRATED

NOTES:

{ DATE: }

"An optimist is someone who thinks that taking a step backward after taking a step forward is not a disaster, it's a cha-cha."

—ROBERT BRAULT

1⊙-MINUTE LIFE CHANGERS

Squeeze in these mini but mighty challenges to speed your results and feel great.

SET YOURSELF UP FOR SUCCESS: Write down your three biggest goals for today.

1 _____

2 _____

3 _____

1O-MINUTE RECHARGE

What _____ ⊙ _____

NOTES: _____

_____

_____

_____

_____

_____

_____

_____

TONING TRACKER _____ ☐ Yes, I did my Fit in 10 workout!

TODAY'S WORKOUT:

WORKOUT NOTES: How did you feel today? What progress are you making when it comes to your strength and fitness goals? Jot it down here.

_____

_____

FOOD TRACKER _____

BREAKFAST: _____

SNACK: _____

LUNCH: _____

DINNER: _____

SNACK: _____

WATER TRACKER _____

Aim to drink ten 8-ounce glasses of H_2O each day. Cross them off as you go!

MOOD TRACKER _____

How are you feeling today? Circle any that apply and make notes below.

HAPPY PROUD FOCUSED ENERGIZED STRONG SAD TIRED FRUSTRATED

NOTES: _____

_____

{ **DATE:** }

"Good things come to those who wait, but better things come to those who go out and get them."

—UNKNOWN

](◔-MINUTE LIFE CHANGERS

Squeeze in these mini but mighty challenges to speed your results and feel great.

SET YOURSELF UP FOR SUCCESS: Write down your three biggest goals for today.

1 _____

2 _____

3 _____

IO-MINUTE RECHARGE

What _____ ◔ _____

NOTES: _____

_____

_____

_____

_____

_____

_____

fit in 10 TONING TRACKER _____ ☐ Yes, I did my Fit in 10 workout!

TODAY'S WORKOUT: Sizzle and Sculpt

WORKOUT NOTES: How did you feel today? What progress are you making when it comes to your strength and fitness goals? Jot it down here.

_____

_____

fit in 10 FOOD TRACKER _____

BREAKFAST: _____

SNACK: _____

LUNCH: _____

DINNER: _____

SNACK: _____

fit in 10 WATER TRACKER _____

Aim to drink ten 8-ounce glasses of H_2O each day. Cross them off as you go!

fit in 10 MOOD TRACKER _____

How are you feeling today? Circle any that apply and make notes below.

HAPPY   PROUD   FOCUSED   ENERGIZED   STRONG   SAD   TIRED   FRUSTRATED

NOTES: _____

_____

{ DATE: }

"It is not in the stars to hold our destiny, but in ourselves."

—WILLIAM SHAKESPEARE

1⊘-MINUTE LIFE CHANGERS

Squeeze in these mini but mighty challenges to speed your results and feel great.

SET YOURSELF UP FOR SUCCESS: Write down your three biggest goals for today.

1 _____

2 _____

3 _____

10-MINUTE RECHARGE

What _____ ⊘ _____

NOTES: _____

_____

_____

_____

_____

_____

_____

fit in 10 TONING TRACKER _____ ☐ Yes, I did my Fit in 10 workout!

TODAY'S WORKOUT: Deep Core

WORKOUT NOTES: How did you feel today? What progress are you making when it comes to your strength and fitness goals? Jot it down here.

_____

_____

fit in 10 FOOD TRACKER _____

BREAKFAST: _____

SNACK: _____

LUNCH: _____

DINNER: _____

SNACK: _____

fit in 10 WATER TRACKER _____

Aim to drink ten 8-ounce glasses of H_2O each day. Cross them off as you go!

fit in 10 MOOD TRACKER _____

How are you feeling today? Circle any that apply and make notes below.

| HAPPY | PROUD | FOCUSED | ENERGIZED | STRONG | SAD | TIRED | FRUSTRATED |

NOTES: _____

_____

_____

{ DATE: }

"I am going to be strong today. I tried it yesterday and I think I am hooked."

—NEILA REY

10-MINUTE LIFE CHANGERS

Squeeze in these mini but mighty challenges to speed your results and feel great.

SET YOURSELF UP FOR SUCCESS : Write down your three biggest goals for today.

1 _____

2 _____

3 _____

10-MINUTE RECHARGE

What _____ 🕐 _____

NOTES: _____

_____

_____

_____

_____

_____

_____

_____

_____

fit IN 10 TONING TRACKER

☐ Yes, I did my Fit in 10 workout!

TODAY'S WORKOUT: Happy Hipster

WORKOUT NOTES: How did you feel today? What progress are you making when it comes to your strength and fitness goals? Jot it down here.

_____

_____

fit IN 10 FOOD TRACKER

BREAKFAST: _____

SNACK: _____

LUNCH: _____

DINNER: _____

SNACK: _____

fit IN 10 WATER TRACKER

Aim to drink ten 8-ounce glasses of H$_2$O each day. Cross them off as you go!

fit IN 10 MOOD TRACKER

How are you feeling today? Circle any that apply and make notes below.

HAPPY   PROUD   FOCUSED   ENERGIZED   STRONG   SAD   TIRED   FRUSTRATED

NOTES: _____

_____

{ DATE: }

"You can never cross the ocean until you have the courage to lose sight of the shore."

—CHRISTOPHER COLUMBUS

1⏲-MINUTE LIFE CHANGERS

Squeeze in these mini but mighty challenges to speed your results and feel great.

SET YOURSELF UP FOR SUCCESS: Write down your three biggest goals for today.

1 _____

2 _____

3 _____

1O-MINUTE RECHARGE

What _____ ⏲ _____

NOTES: _____

_____

_____

_____

_____

_____

_____

_____

_____

fit in 10 TONING TRACKER

☐ Yes, I did my Fit in 10 workout!

TODAY'S WORKOUT: Back to Strong

WORKOUT NOTES: How did you feel today? What progress are you making when it comes to your strength and fitness goals? Jot it down here.

_____

_____

fit in 10 FOOD TRACKER

BREAKFAST: _____

SNACK: _____

LUNCH: _____

DINNER: _____

SNACK: _____

fit in 10 WATER TRACKER

Aim to drink ten 8-ounce glasses of H_2O each day. Cross them off as you go!

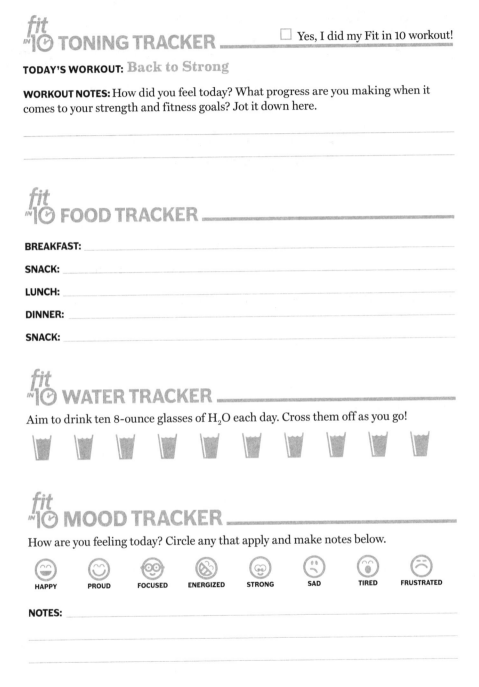

fit in 10 MOOD TRACKER

How are you feeling today? Circle any that apply and make notes below.

HAPPY   PROUD   FOCUSED   ENERGIZED   STRONG   SAD   TIRED   FRUSTRATED

NOTES: _____

_____

_____

{ DATE: }

"I have not failed. I've just found 10,000 ways that won't work."

—THOMAS EDISON

1◷-MINUTE LIFE CHANGERS

Squeeze in these mini but mighty challenges to speed your results and feel great.

SET YOURSELF UP FOR SUCCESS: Write down your three biggest goals for today.

1 _____

2 _____

3 _____

10-MINUTE RECHARGE

What _____ ◷ _____

NOTES: _____

_____

_____

_____

_____

_____

_____

_____

fit IN 10 TONING TRACKER

☐ Yes, I did my Fit in 10 workout!

TODAY'S WORKOUT: Flat and Firm Abs

WORKOUT NOTES: How did you feel today? What progress are you making when it comes to your strength and fitness goals? Jot it down here.

_____

_____

fit IN 10 FOOD TRACKER

BREAKFAST: _____

SNACK: _____

LUNCH: _____

DINNER: _____

SNACK: _____

fit IN 10 WATER TRACKER

Aim to drink ten 8-ounce glasses of H_2O each day. Cross them off as you go!

fit IN 10 MOOD TRACKER

How are you feeling today? Circle any that apply and make notes below.

| HAPPY | PROUD | FOCUSED | ENERGIZED | STRONG | SAD | TIRED | FRUSTRATED |

NOTES: _____

_____

_____

{ DATE: }

"Be yourself. Everyone else is already taken."

—OSCAR WILDE

1ⓒ-MINUTE LIFE CHANGERS

Squeeze in these mini but mighty challenges to speed your results and feel great.

SET YOURSELF UP FOR SUCCESS: Write down your three biggest goals for today.

1 _____

2 _____

3 _____

1O-MINUTE RECHARGE

What _____ ⓒ _____

NOTES: _____

_____

_____

_____

_____

_____

_____

_____

fit in 10 TONING TRACKER

☐ Yes, I did my Fit in 10 workout!

TODAY'S WORKOUT: Meta Blast

WORKOUT NOTES: How did you feel today? What progress are you making when it comes to your strength and fitness goals? Jot it down here.

_____

_____

fit in 10 FOOD TRACKER

BREAKFAST: _____

SNACK: _____

LUNCH: _____

DINNER: _____

SNACK: _____

fit in 10 WATER TRACKER

Aim to drink ten 8-ounce glasses of H_2O each day. Cross them off as you go!

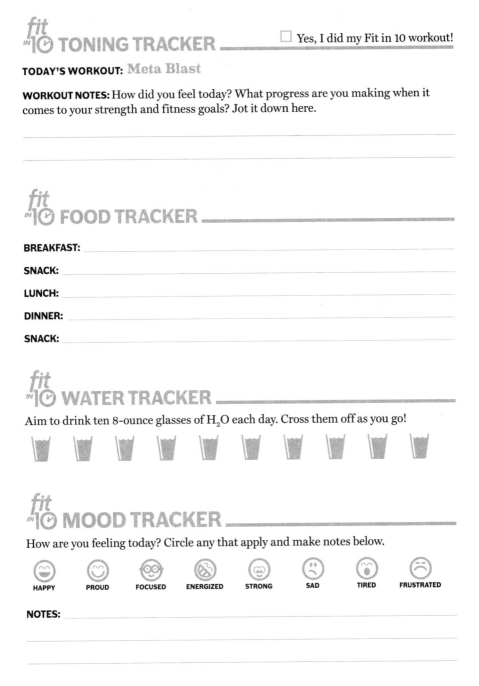

fit in 10 MOOD TRACKER

How are you feeling today? Circle any that apply and make notes below.

HAPPY   PROUD   FOCUSED   ENERGIZED   STRONG   SAD   TIRED   FRUSTRATED

NOTES: _____

_____

{ **DATE:** }

*"I celebrate myself,
and sing myself."*

—WALT WHITMAN

1⊘-MINUTE LIFE CHANGERS

Squeeze in these mini but mighty challenges to speed your results and feel great.

SET YOURSELF UP FOR SUCCESS: Write down your three biggest goals for today.

1 _____

2 _____

3 _____

10-MINUTE RECHARGE

What _____ 🕐 _____

NOTES: _____

_____

_____

_____

_____

_____

_____

_____

fit in 10 TONING TRACKER

☐ Yes, I did my Fit in 10 workout!

TODAY'S WORKOUT: Lean and Lovely Legs

WORKOUT NOTES: How did you feel today? What progress are you making when it comes to your strength and fitness goals? Jot it down here.

_____

_____

fit in 10 FOOD TRACKER

BREAKFAST: _____

SNACK: _____

LUNCH: _____

DINNER: _____

SNACK: _____

fit in 10 WATER TRACKER

Aim to drink ten 8-ounce glasses of H_2O each day. Cross them off as you go!

fit in 10 MOOD TRACKER

How are you feeling today? Circle any that apply and make notes below.

HAPPY   PROUD   FOCUSED   ENERGIZED   STRONG   SAD   TIRED   FRUSTRATED

NOTES: _____

_____

Cycle
3

DAYS 21–30

*"No one can make
you feel inferior without
your consent."*

—ELEANOR ROOSEVELT

Welcome to your third cycle of the Fit in 10 Plan! Hopefully by now you're feeling stronger, leaner, and more energized. As we move into cycle 3, we'll continue to up the intensity of your Fit in 10 routines. Make sure to challenge yourself, and that by the end of those 10 minutes your heart is pumping and you've broken a sweat. Perhaps you can start using a thicker resistance band or grab heavier dumbbells.

We'll also be adding in another 10-Minute Life Changer to help you optimize your life in other ways, just 10 minutes at a time. Ready? Let's get started!

1⊘-MINUTE LIFE CHANGER
Have a Mindful Meal

The goal for this cycle is to slow down when you chow down. According to the British Nutrition Foundation, it takes about 20 minutes for your stomach to signal to your brain that it's full. So if you're scarfing down an entire meal, say, in less than 5 minutes, you're more likely to go up for seconds—or thirds—because you're not taking the time to think about if you're actually hungry for more. A study published in the *British Medical Journal* reports that people who eat quickly have a tripled risk of being overweight than those who eat more slowly.

Starting today, aim to take at least 10 minutes to sit down, eat, and enjoy one of your meals. Notice the smell, taste, and texture of every bite. We know everyone has a busy schedule, so you pick the meal: breakfast, lunch, or dinner. You'll see a place in your Fit in 10 journal to mark this challenge after it's complete—make sure to write down the meal(s) where you took at least 10 minutes to eat, bonus points for dining longer! As you become more used to eating mindfully, try to eat more slowly at every meal. You'll be surprised by how much enjoyment you were missing out on during mealtime before!

{ DATE: }

"Little by little does the trick."

—AESOP

―――――――― 1⏱-MINUTE LIFE CHANGERS ――――――――

Squeeze in these mini but mighty challenges to speed your results and feel great.

SET YOURSELF UP FOR SUCCESS: Write down your three biggest goals for today.

1 _____

2 _____

3 _____

10-MINUTE RECHARGE

What _____ 🕐 _____

10-MINUTE MINDFUL MEAL

What _____ 🕐 _____

NOTES: _____

_____

_____

_____

_____

_____

fit 10 TONING TRACKER _____ ☐ Yes, I did my Fit in 10 workout!

TODAY'S WORKOUT: Flat and Firm Abs

WORKOUT NOTES: How did you feel today? What progress are you making when it comes to your strength and fitness goals? Jot it down here.

_____

_____

fit 10 FOOD TRACKER _____

BREAKFAST: _____

SNACK: _____

LUNCH: _____

DINNER: _____

SNACK: _____

fit 10 WATER TRACKER _____

Aim to drink ten 8-ounce glasses of H$_2$O each day. Cross them off as you go!

fit 10 MOOD TRACKER _____

How are you feeling today? Circle any that apply and make notes below.

HAPPY   PROUD   FOCUSED   ENERGIZED   STRONG   SAD   TIRED   FRUSTRATED

NOTES: _____

_____

_____

{ DATE: }

"Light tomorrow with today."

—ELIZABETH BARRETT BROWNING

1Ⓒ-MINUTE LIFE CHANGERS

Squeeze in these mini but mighty challenges to speed your results and feel great.

SET YOURSELF UP FOR SUCCESS: Write down your three biggest goals for today.

1 _____

2 _____

3 _____

10-MINUTE RECHARGE

What _____ Ⓒ _____

10-MINUTE MINDFUL MEAL

What _____ Ⓒ _____

NOTES: _____

_____

_____

_____

_____

_____

fit IN 10 TONING TRACKER

☐ Yes, I did my Fit in 10 workout!

TODAY'S WORKOUT: Ultimate Booty Lifter

WORKOUT NOTES: How did you feel today? What progress are you making when it comes to your strength and fitness goals? Jot it down here.

_____

_____

fit IN 10 FOOD TRACKER

BREAKFAST: _____

SNACK: _____

LUNCH: _____

DINNER: _____

SNACK: _____

fit IN 10 WATER TRACKER

Aim to drink ten 8-ounce glasses of H_2O each day. Cross them off as you go!

fit IN 10 MOOD TRACKER

How are you feeling today? Circle any that apply and make notes below.

😄 HAPPY   😊 PROUD   🤓 FOCUSED   😎 ENERGIZED   😁 STRONG   🙁 SAD   😮 TIRED   😣 FRUSTRATED

NOTES: _____

_____

{ DATE: }

*"It does not matter how slowly you go
as long as you do not stop."*

—CONFUCIUS

1⦵-MINUTE LIFE CHANGERS

Squeeze in these mini but mighty challenges to speed your results and feel great.

SET YOURSELF UP FOR SUCCESS : Write down your three biggest goals for today.

1 _____

2 _____

3 _____

10-MINUTE RECHARGE

What _____ 🕑 _____

10-MINUTE MINDFUL MEAL

What _____ 🕑 _____

NOTES: _____

_____

_____

_____

_____

_____

fit in 10 TONING TRACKER _____ ☐ Yes, I did my Fit in 10 workout!

TODAY'S WORKOUT: Totally Toned Triceps

WORKOUT NOTES: How did you feel today? What progress are you making when it comes to your strength and fitness goals? Jot it down here.

_____

_____

fit in 10 FOOD TRACKER _____

BREAKFAST: _____

SNACK: _____

LUNCH: _____

DINNER: _____

SNACK: _____

fit in 10 WATER TRACKER _____

Aim to drink ten 8-ounce glasses of H_2O each day. Cross them off as you go!

🥛 🥛 🥛 🥛 🥛 🥛 🥛 🥛 🥛 🥛

fit in 10 MOOD TRACKER _____

How are you feeling today? Circle any that apply and make notes below.

😄   😊   🤓   😎   😁   🙁   😮   😖

HAPPY   **PROUD**   **FOCUSED**   **ENERGIZED**   **STRONG**   **SAD**   **TIRED**   **FRUSTRATED**

NOTES: _____

_____

_____

{ DATE: }

"It's not what you look at that matters, it's what you see."

—HENRY DAVID THOREAU

1⏱-MINUTE LIFE CHANGERS

Squeeze in these mini but mighty challenges to speed your results and feel great.

SET YOURSELF UP FOR SUCCESS: Write down your three biggest goals for today.

1 _____

2 _____

3 _____

10-MINUTE RECHARGE

What _____ ⏱ _____

10-MINUTE MINDFUL MEAL

What _____ ⏱ _____

NOTES: _____

_____

_____

_____

_____

_____

fit IN 10 TONING TRACKER ☐ Yes, I did my Fit in 10 workout!

TODAY'S WORKOUT: Torch to Tone

WORKOUT NOTES: How did you feel today? What progress are you making when it comes to your strength and fitness goals? Jot it down here.

_____

_____

fit IN 10 FOOD TRACKER

BREAKFAST: _____

SNACK: _____

LUNCH: _____

DINNER: _____

SNACK: _____

fit IN 10 WATER TRACKER

Aim to drink ten 8-ounce glasses of H_2O each day. Cross them off as you go!

fit IN 10 MOOD TRACKER

How are you feeling today? Circle any that apply and make notes below.

HAPPY   PROUD   FOCUSED   ENERGIZED   STRONG   SAD   TIRED   FRUSTRATED

NOTES: _____

_____

{ DATE: }

*"Not life, but good life,
is to be chiefly valued."*

—SOCRATES

1⦾-MINUTE LIFE CHANGERS

Squeeze in these mini but mighty challenges to speed your results and feel great.

SET YOURSELF UP FOR SUCCESS: Write down your three biggest goals for today.

1 _____

2 _____

3 _____

1O-MINUTE RECHARGE

What _____ 🕑 _____

1O-MINUTE MINDFUL MEAL

What _____ 🕑 _____

NOTES: _____

_____

_____

_____

_____

_____

fit IN 10 TONING TRACKER

☐ Yes, I did my Fit in 10 workout!

TODAY'S WORKOUT: Back to Strong

WORKOUT NOTES: How did you feel today? What progress are you making when it comes to your strength and fitness goals? Jot it down here.

fit IN 10 FOOD TRACKER

BREAKFAST:

SNACK:

LUNCH:

DINNER:

SNACK:

fit IN 10 WATER TRACKER

Aim to drink ten 8-ounce glasses of H_2O each day. Cross them off as you go!

fit IN 10 MOOD TRACKER

How are you feeling today? Circle any that apply and make notes below.

HAPPY   PROUD   FOCUSED   ENERGIZED   STRONG   SAD   TIRED   FRUSTRATED

NOTES:

{ **DATE:** }

*"Be not afraid of growing slowly,
be afraid only of standing still."*

—CHINESE PROVERB

1⊙-MINUTE LIFE CHANGERS

Squeeze in these mini but mighty challenges to speed your results and feel great.

SET YOURSELF UP FOR SUCCESS : Write down your three biggest goals for today.

1 _____

2 _____

3 _____

10-MINUTE RECHARGE

What _____ ⊙ _____

10-MINUTE MINDFUL MEAL

What _____ ⊙ _____

NOTES: _____

_____

_____

_____

_____

_____

fit IN**10** TONING TRACKER

☐ Yes, I did my Fit in 10 workout!

TODAY'S WORKOUT: *Sizzle and Sculpt*

WORKOUT NOTES: How did you feel today? What progress are you making when it comes to your strength and fitness goals? Jot it down here.

fit IN**10** FOOD TRACKER

BREAKFAST:

SNACK:

LUNCH:

DINNER:

SNACK:

fit IN**10** WATER TRACKER

Aim to drink ten 8-ounce glasses of H_2O each day. Cross them off as you go!

fit IN**10** MOOD TRACKER

How are you feeling today? Circle any that apply and make notes below.

HAPPY   PROUD   FOCUSED   ENERGIZED   STRONG   SAD   TIRED   FRUSTRATED

NOTES:

{ **DATE:** }

"Optimism is the faith that leads to achievement."

—HELEN KELLER

1⊘-MINUTE LIFE CHANGERS

Squeeze in these mini but mighty challenges to speed your results and feel great.

SET YOURSELF UP FOR SUCCESS : Write down your three biggest goals for today.

1 _____

2 _____

3 _____

10-MINUTE RECHARGE

What _____ ⊙ _____

10-MINUTE MINDFUL MEAL

What _____ ⊙ _____

NOTES: _____

_____

_____

_____

_____

_____

fit IN 10 TONING TRACKER _____ ☐ Yes, I did my Fit in 10 workout!

TODAY'S WORKOUT: Dare to Bare Arms + Deep Core*

WORKOUT NOTES: How did you feel today? What progress are you making when it comes to your strength and fitness goals? Jot it down here.

_____

_____

fit IN 10 FOOD TRACKER _____

BREAKFAST: _____

SNACK: _____

LUNCH: _____

DINNER: _____

SNACK: _____

fit IN 10 WATER TRACKER _____

Aim to drink ten 8-ounce glasses of H_2O each day. Cross them off as you go!

fit IN 10 MOOD TRACKER _____

How are you feeling today? Circle any that apply and make notes below.

| HAPPY | PROUD | FOCUSED | ENERGIZED | STRONG | SAD | TIRED | FRUSTRATED |

NOTES: _____

_____

*optional

{ **DATE:** }

"The universe is full of magical things patiently waiting for our wits to grow sharper."

—EDEN PHILLPOTTS

1⊘-MINUTE LIFE CHANGERS

Squeeze in these mini but mighty challenges to speed your results and feel great.

SET YOURSELF UP FOR SUCCESS: Write down your three biggest goals for today.

1 _____

2 _____

3 _____

10-MINUTE RECHARGE

What _____ 🕐 _____

10-MINUTE MINDFUL MEAL

What _____ 🕐 _____

NOTES: _____

_____

_____

_____

_____

_____

fit in 10 TONING TRACKER _____

☐ Yes, I did my Fit in 10 workout!

TODAY'S WORKOUT: Happy Hipster

WORKOUT NOTES: How did you feel today? What progress are you making when it comes to your strength and fitness goals? Jot it down here.

_____

_____

fit in 10 FOOD TRACKER _____

BREAKFAST: _____

SNACK: _____

LUNCH: _____

DINNER: _____

SNACK: _____

fit in 10 WATER TRACKER _____

Aim to drink ten 8-ounce glasses of H_2O each day. Cross them off as you go!

fit in 10 MOOD TRACKER _____

How are you feeling today? Circle any that apply and make notes below.

HAPPY PROUD FOCUSED ENERGIZED STRONG SAD TIRED FRUSTRATED

NOTES: _____

_____

_____

{ DATE: }

*"It takes more than just a good-looking body.
You've got to have the heart and soul to go with it."*

—EPICTETUS

1⏲-MINUTE LIFE CHANGERS

Squeeze in these mini but mighty challenges to speed your results and feel great.

SET YOURSELF UP FOR SUCCESS: Write down your three biggest goals for today.

1 _____

2 _____

3 _____

10-MINUTE RECHARGE

What _____ ⏲ _____

10-MINUTE MINDFUL MEAL

What _____ ⏲ _____

NOTES: _____

_____

_____

_____

_____

_____

fit in 10 TONING TRACKER

☐ Yes, I did my Fit in 10 workout!

TODAY'S WORKOUT: Tummy Love

WORKOUT NOTES: How did you feel today? What progress are you making when it comes to your strength and fitness goals? Jot it down here.

fit in 10 FOOD TRACKER

BREAKFAST:

SNACK:

LUNCH:

DINNER:

SNACK:

fit in 10 WATER TRACKER

Aim to drink ten 8-ounce glasses of H_2O each day. Cross them off as you go!

fit in 10 MOOD TRACKER

How are you feeling today? Circle any that apply and make notes below.

HAPPY · PROUD · FOCUSED · ENERGIZED · STRONG · SAD · TIRED · FRUSTRATED

NOTES:

{ DATE: }

*"When I let go of what I am,
I become what I might be."*

—LAO TZU

1Ⓞ-MINUTE LIFE CHANGERS

Squeeze in these mini but mighty challenges to speed your results and feel great.

SET YOURSELF UP FOR SUCCESS: Write down your three biggest goals for today.

1 _____

2 _____

3 _____

1O-MINUTE RECHARGE

What _____ 🕐 _____

1O-MINUTE MINDFUL MEAL

What _____ 🕐 _____

NOTES: _____

_____

_____

_____

_____

_____

 **TONING TRACKER** ☐ Yes, I did my Fit in 10 workout!

TODAY'S WORKOUT: Meta Blast

WORKOUT NOTES: How did you feel today? What progress are you making when it comes to your strength and fitness goals? Jot it down here.

_____

_____

 **FOOD TRACKER**

BREAKFAST: _____

SNACK: _____

LUNCH: _____

DINNER: _____

SNACK: _____

WATER TRACKER

Aim to drink ten 8-ounce glasses of H_2O each day. Cross them off as you go!

MOOD TRACKER

How are you feeling today? Circle any that apply and make notes below.

HAPPY   PROUD   FOCUSED   ENERGIZED   STRONG   SAD   TIRED   FRUSTRATED

NOTES: _____

_____

_____

Cycle
4

DAYS 31–40

"It's not about time, it's about choices. How are you spending your choices?"

—BEVERLY ADAMO

Welcome to cycle 4 of the Fit in 10 Plan! You should feel proud that you're already halfway through the 60-day program and that you're changing your life and body just 10 minutes at a time—how cool is that?

By now, you're probably starting to notice even more changes in your health and body. Hopefully you're sleeping better and waking up with more energy. Perhaps it's easier to run up the stairs or pick up the laundry basket. Maybe you're even starting to see the beginning of a bicep or the curve of your waist. Whatever changes, whether they're big or small, they're awesome and worth celebrating. Consider giving yourself a healthy reward, like a new exercise top or sneakers. You deserve it!

Then, get ready to see even more changes over the next 10 days. We'll continue to increase the challenge of the Fit in 10 routines, so make sure you modify exercises when needed and pick up heavier weights or resistance bands when you feel ready. Remember to write down your meals so you continue to feed your muscles and fire up your metabolism.

We're also adding a new 10-Minute Life Changer, so make sure to check it out below and commit to doing it daily. You've got this!

10-MINUTE LIFE CHANGER
Take a 10-Minute Walk

While your 10-minute Fit in 10 routines will transform your body, it's not healthy to sit the rest of the day. So the goal for this week is to walk for just 10 minutes more each day. A study published in the *American Journal of Preventive Medicine* shows that women who walk and have high levels of physical activity have a better quality of life in the areas of physical functioning, vitality, and social settings.

Bonus if you can take your walk outside with a friend—a study published in *Ecopsychology* says walking in a group in nature can significantly lower depression, diminish stress, and enhance mental health.

{ DATE: }

"The groundwork of all happiness is health."

—LEIGH HUNT

───── 1⏱-MINUTE LIFE CHANGERS ─────

Squeeze in these mini but mighty challenges to speed your results and feel great.

SET YOURSELF UP FOR SUCCESS : Write down your three biggest goals for today.

1 _____

2 _____

3 _____

10-MINUTE RECHARGE

What _____ 🕑 _____

10-MINUTE MINDFUL MEAL

What _____ 🕑 _____

10-MINUTE WALK

Where _____ 🕑 _____

NOTES: _____

_____

_____

_____

fit IN 10 TONING TRACKER _____ ☐ Yes, I did my Fit in 10 workout!

TODAY'S WORKOUT: Lean and Lovely Legs

WORKOUT NOTES: How did you feel today? What progress are you making when it comes to your strength and fitness goals? Jot it down here.

_____

_____

fit IN 10 FOOD TRACKER _____

BREAKFAST: _____

SNACK: _____

LUNCH: _____

DINNER: _____

SNACK: _____

fit IN 10 WATER TRACKER _____

Aim to drink ten 8-ounce glasses of H_2O each day. Cross them off as you go!

🥛 🥛 🥛 🥛 🥛 🥛 🥛 🥛 🥛 🥛

fit IN 10 MOOD TRACKER _____

How are you feeling today? Circle any that apply and make notes below.

😄 😊 🤓 😎 😁 🙁 😫 😣
HAPPY   PROUD   FOCUSED   ENERGIZED   STRONG   SAD   TIRED   FRUSTRATED

NOTES: _____

_____

_____

{ DATE: }

*"Act as if what you do
makes a difference. It does."*

—WILLIAM JAMES

1⏱-MINUTE LIFE CHANGERS

Squeeze in these mini but mighty challenges to speed your results and feel great.

SET YOURSELF UP FOR SUCCESS: Write down your three biggest goals for today.

1 _____

2 _____

3 _____

1O-MINUTE RECHARGE

What _____ ⏱ _____

1O-MINUTE MINDFUL MEAL

What _____ ⏱ _____

1O-MINUTE WALK

Where _____ ⏱ _____

NOTES: _____

_____

_____

_____

fit in 10 **TONING TRACKER**

TODAY'S WORKOUT: Totally Toned Triceps

WORKOUT NOTES: How did you feel today? What progress are you making when it comes to your strength and fitness goals? Jot it down here.

_____

_____

fit in 10 **FOOD TRACKER**

BREAKFAST: _____

SNACK: _____

LUNCH: _____

DINNER: _____

SNACK: _____

fit in 10 **WATER TRACKER**

Aim to drink ten 8-ounce glasses of H_2O each day. Cross them off as you go!

fit in 10 **MOOD TRACKER**

How are you feeling today? Circle any that apply and make notes below.

HAPPY PROUD FOCUSED ENERGIZED STRONG SAD TIRED FRUSTRATED

NOTES: _____

_____

_____

{ DATE: }

"I may not be there yet, but I'm closer than I was yesterday."
—UNKNOWN

1🕐-MINUTE LIFE CHANGERS

Squeeze in these mini but mighty challenges to speed your results and feel great.

SET YOURSELF UP FOR SUCCESS: Write down your three biggest goals for today.

1 _____

2 _____

3 _____

10-MINUTE RECHARGE

What _____ 🕐 _____

10-MINUTE MINDFUL MEAL

What _____ 🕐 _____

10-MINUTE WALK

Where _____ 🕐 _____

NOTES: _____

_____

_____

_____

 **TONING TRACKER** _____ ☐ Yes, I did my Fit in 10 workout!

TODAY'S WORKOUT: Sizzle and Sculpt

WORKOUT NOTES: How did you feel today? What progress are you making when it comes to your strength and fitness goals? Jot it down here.

_____

_____

FOOD TRACKER _____

BREAKFAST: _____

SNACK: _____

LUNCH: _____

DINNER: _____

SNACK: _____

WATER TRACKER _____

Aim to drink ten 8-ounce glasses of H_2O each day. Cross them off as you go!

MOOD TRACKER _____

How are you feeling today? Circle any that apply and make notes below.

HAPPY   **PROUD**   **FOCUSED**   **ENERGIZED**   **STRONG**   **SAD**   **TIRED**   **FRUSTRATED**

NOTES: _____

_____

_____

{ DATE: }

*"What seems to us as bitter trials
are often blessings in disguise."*

—OSCAR WILDE

1⊘-MINUTE LIFE CHANGERS

Squeeze in these mini but mighty challenges to speed your results and feel great.

SET YOURSELF UP FOR SUCCESS: Write down your three biggest goals for today.

1 _____

2 _____

3 _____

10-MINUTE RECHARGE

What _____ ⊘ _____

10-MINUTE MINDFUL MEAL

What _____ ⊘ _____

10-MINUTE WALK

Where _____ ⊘ _____

NOTES: _____

_____

_____

_____

fit in 10 TONING TRACKER

☐ Yes, I did my Fit in 10 workout!

TODAY'S WORKOUT: Back to Strong + Deep Core*

WORKOUT NOTES: How did you feel today? What progress are you making when it comes to your strength and fitness goals? Jot it down here.

fit in 10 FOOD TRACKER

BREAKFAST:

SNACK:

LUNCH:

DINNER:

SNACK:

fit in 10 WATER TRACKER

Aim to drink ten 8-ounce glasses of H_2O each day. Cross them off as you go!

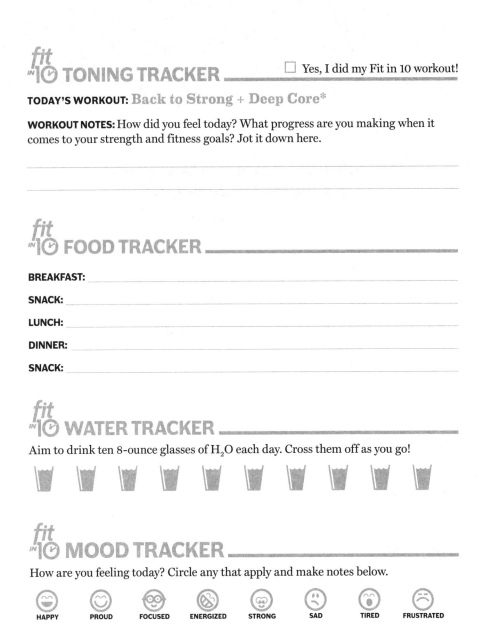

fit in 10 MOOD TRACKER

How are you feeling today? Circle any that apply and make notes below.

HAPPY   PROUD   FOCUSED   ENERGIZED   STRONG   SAD   TIRED   FRUSTRATED

NOTES:

*optional

{ DATE: }

*"The only person you are destined to become
is the person you decide to be."*

—RALPH WALDO EMERSON

1⊘-MINUTE LIFE CHANGERS

Squeeze in these mini but mighty challenges to speed your results and feel great.

SET YOURSELF UP FOR SUCCESS: Write down your three biggest goals for today.

1 _____

2 _____

3 _____

10-MINUTE RECHARGE

What _____ 🕑 _____

10-MINUTE MINDFUL MEAL

What _____ 🕑 _____

10-MINUTE WALK

Where _____ 🕑 _____

NOTES: _____

_____

_____

_____

fit in 10 TONING TRACKER ☐ Yes, I did my Fit in 10 workout!

TODAY'S WORKOUT: Ultimate Booty Lifter

WORKOUT NOTES: How did you feel today? What progress are you making when it comes to your strength and fitness goals? Jot it down here.

_____

_____

fit in 10 FOOD TRACKER

BREAKFAST: _____

SNACK: _____

LUNCH: _____

DINNER: _____

SNACK: _____

fit in 10 WATER TRACKER

Aim to drink ten 8-ounce glasses of H_2O each day. Cross them off as you go!

fit in 10 MOOD TRACKER

How are you feeling today? Circle any that apply and make notes below.

HAPPY   PROUD   FOCUSED   ENERGIZED   STRONG   SAD   TIRED   FRUSTRATED

NOTES: _____

_____

{ DATE: }

*"We are what we think. All that
we are arises with our thoughts. With
our thoughts we make the world."*

—BUDDHA

1⊘-MINUTE LIFE CHANGERS

Squeeze in these mini but mighty challenges to speed your results and feel great.

SET YOURSELF UP FOR SUCCESS : Write down your three biggest goals for today.

1 _____

2 _____

3 _____

10-MINUTE RECHARGE

What _____ ⊘ _____

10-MINUTE MINDFUL MEAL

What _____ ⊘ _____

10-MINUTE WALK

Where _____ ⊘ _____

NOTES: _____

_____

_____

_____

fit IN 10 TONING TRACKER

☐ Yes, I did my Fit in 10 workout!

TODAY'S WORKOUT: Meta Blast

WORKOUT NOTES: How did you feel today? What progress are you making when it comes to your strength and fitness goals? Jot it down here.

_____

_____

fit IN 10 FOOD TRACKER

BREAKFAST: _____

SNACK: _____

LUNCH: _____

DINNER: _____

SNACK: _____

fit IN 10 WATER TRACKER

Aim to drink ten 8-ounce glasses of H_2O each day. Cross them off as you go!

fit IN 10 MOOD TRACKER

How are you feeling today? Circle any that apply and make notes below.

HAPPY   PROUD   FOCUSED   ENERGIZED   STRONG   SAD   TIRED   FRUSTRATED

NOTES: _____

_____

_____

{ DATE: }

"I like the dreams of the future better than the history of the past."

—THOMAS JEFFERSON

10-MINUTE LIFE CHANGERS

Squeeze in these mini but mighty challenges to speed your results and feel great.

SET YOURSELF UP FOR SUCCESS: Write down your three biggest goals for today.

1 _____

2 _____

3 _____

10-MINUTE RECHARGE

What _____ 🕐 _____

10-MINUTE MINDFUL MEAL

What _____ 🕐 _____

10-MINUTE WALK

Where _____ 🕐 _____

NOTES: _____

_____

_____

_____

fit IN 10 TONING TRACKER _____

☐ Yes, I did my Fit in 10 workout!

TODAY'S WORKOUT: Dare to Bare Arms

WORKOUT NOTES: How did you feel today? What progress are you making when it comes to your strength and fitness goals? Jot it down here.

_____

_____

fit IN 10 FOOD TRACKER _____

BREAKFAST: _____

SNACK: _____

LUNCH: _____

DINNER: _____

SNACK: _____

fit IN 10 WATER TRACKER _____

Aim to drink ten 8-ounce glasses of H_2O each day. Cross them off as you go!

fit IN 10 MOOD TRACKER _____

How are you feeling today? Circle any that apply and make notes below.

HAPPY   PROUD   FOCUSED   ENERGIZED   STRONG   SAD   TIRED   FRUSTRATED

NOTES: _____

_____

_____

{ DATE: }

"Always do what you are afraid to do."

—RALPH WALDO EMERSON

10-MINUTE LIFE CHANGERS

Squeeze in these mini but mighty challenges to speed your results and feel great.

SET YOURSELF UP FOR SUCCESS : Write down your three biggest goals for today.

1 _____

2 _____

3 _____

10-MINUTE RECHARGE

What _____ 🕐 _____

10-MINUTE MINDFUL MEAL

What _____ 🕐 _____

10-MINUTE WALK

Where _____ 🕐 _____

NOTES: _____

_____

_____

_____

fit IN 10 TONING TRACKER _____ ☐ Yes, I did my Fit in 10 workout!

TODAY'S WORKOUT: Happy Hipster

WORKOUT NOTES: How did you feel today? What progress are you making when it comes to your strength and fitness goals? Jot it down here.

_____

_____

fit IN 10 FOOD TRACKER _____

BREAKFAST: _____

SNACK: _____

LUNCH: _____

DINNER: _____

SNACK: _____

fit IN 10 WATER TRACKER _____

Aim to drink ten 8-ounce glasses of H_2O each day. Cross them off as you go!

fit IN 10 MOOD TRACKER _____

How are you feeling today? Circle any that apply and make notes below.

HAPPY   **PROUD**   **FOCUSED**   **ENERGIZED**   **STRONG**   **SAD**   **TIRED**   **FRUSTRATED**

NOTES: _____

_____

_____

{ DATE: }

*"It's never too late to become
what you might have been."*

—GEORGE ELIOT

10-MINUTE LIFE CHANGERS

Squeeze in these mini but mighty challenges to speed your results and feel great.

SET YOURSELF UP FOR SUCCESS: Write down your three biggest goals for today.

1 _____

2 _____

3 _____

10-MINUTE RECHARGE

What _____ 🕑 _____

10-MINUTE MINDFUL MEAL

What _____ 🕑 _____

10-MINUTE WALK

Where _____ 🕑 _____

NOTES: _____

_____

_____

_____

fit IN 10 TONING TRACKER

☐ Yes, I did my Fit in 10 workout!

TODAY'S WORKOUT: Torch to Tone + Tummy Love*

WORKOUT NOTES: How did you feel today? What progress are you making when it comes to your strength and fitness goals? Jot it down here.

_____

_____

fit IN 10 FOOD TRACKER

BREAKFAST: _____

SNACK: _____

LUNCH: _____

DINNER: _____

SNACK: _____

fit IN 10 WATER TRACKER

Aim to drink ten 8-ounce glasses of H_2O each day. Cross them off as you go!

fit IN 10 MOOD TRACKER

How are you feeling today? Circle any that apply and make notes below.

HAPPY   PROUD   FOCUSED   ENERGIZED   STRONG   SAD   TIRED   FRUSTRATED

NOTES: _____

_____

*optional

97

{ DATE: }

*"Grace is the beauty of form
under the influence of freedom."*

—FRIEDRICH SCHILLER

10-MINUTE LIFE CHANGERS

Squeeze in these mini but mighty challenges to speed your results and feel great.

SET YOURSELF UP FOR SUCCESS: Write down your three biggest goals for today.

1 _____

2 _____

3 _____

10-MINUTE RECHARGE

What _____ 🕑 _____

10-MINUTE MINDFUL MEAL

What _____ 🕑 _____

10-MINUTE WALK

Where _____ 🕑 _____

NOTES: _____

_____

_____

_____

fit TONING TRACKER _____ ☐ Yes, I did my Fit in 10 workout!

TODAY'S WORKOUT: Flat and Firm Abs

WORKOUT NOTES: How did you feel today? What progress are you making when it comes to your strength and fitness goals? Jot it down here.

_____

_____

fit FOOD TRACKER _____

BREAKFAST: _____

SNACK: _____

LUNCH: _____

DINNER: _____

SNACK: _____

fit WATER TRACKER _____

Aim to drink ten 8-ounce glasses of H_2O each day. Cross them off as you go!

fit MOOD TRACKER _____

How are you feeling today? Circle any that apply and make notes below.

| HAPPY | PROUD | FOCUSED | ENERGIZED | STRONG | SAD | TIRED | FRUSTRATED |

NOTES: _____

_____

_____

Cycle
5

DAYS 41–50

*"What's the point of being
alive if you don't at least try to do
something remarkable?"*

—JOHN GREEN

Welcome to cycle 5 of the Fit in 10 Plan! You are 41 days in, and we hope you are starting to feel strong, fierce, and fabulous. By now, the 10-minute workouts and meals have kicked your metabolism into overdrive and your energy levels should be at an all-time high. Perhaps you've noticed the number on the scale going down, and your clothes are getting looser still. Whatever changes you're noticing, make sure to be proud of your progress—and use it to stay motivated for the next 20 days.

Get ready to continue to challenge yourself with the Fit in 10 routines (they'll be a little more difficult this cycle, so make sure to modify when needed) and be sure to stick to your clean eating.

Of course, we'll also be adding a new 10-Minute Life Changer. So check it out, and start to incorporate it into your day. You're worth it!

1◎-MINUTE LIFE CHANGER
Take a Tech Break

How many times did you pick up your phone to check your email or texts in the last 10 minutes? How about your Facebook page? Too many times to count? We thought so. It might seem like it's impossible to take a 10-minute tech break, but as it turns out, even a short screen break can be good for your health. A study from the University of Illinois, published in *Computers in Human Behavior*, suggests a link between time spent on mobile devices and issues like depression, anxiety, and high stress levels.

So for just 10 minutes a day, try taking a digital detox. That's right; no phone, no TV, no tablet—nada! Hopefully, over time, you'll gradually start to decrease your scroll time and increase your productivity.

{ DATE: }

"He who has health, has hope; and he who has hope, has everything."

—THOMAS CARLYLE

10-MINUTE LIFE CHANGERS

Squeeze in these mini but mighty challenges to speed your results and feel great.

SET YOURSELF UP FOR SUCCESS: Write down your three biggest goals for today.

1 _____

2 _____

3 _____

10-MINUTE RECHARGE

What _____ 🕐 _____

10-MINUTE MINDFUL MEAL

What _____ 🕐 _____

10-MINUTE WALK

Where _____ 🕐 _____

10-MINUTE TECH BREAK

What _____ 🕐 _____

NOTES: _____

_____

fit IN 10 TONING TRACKER _____ ☐ Yes, I did my Fit in 10 workout!

TODAY'S WORKOUT: Meta Blast + Deep Core*

WORKOUT NOTES: How did you feel today? What progress are you making when it comes to your strength and fitness goals? Jot it down here.

_____

_____

fit IN 10 FOOD TRACKER _____

BREAKFAST: _____

SNACK: _____

LUNCH: _____

DINNER: _____

SNACK: _____

fit IN 10 WATER TRACKER _____

Aim to drink ten 8-ounce glasses of H_2O each day. Cross them off as you go!

fit IN 10 MOOD TRACKER _____

How are you feeling today? Circle any that apply and make notes below.

HAPPY PROUD FOCUSED ENERGIZED STRONG SAD TIRED FRUSTRATED

NOTES: _____

_____

*optional

{ DATE: }

"The best protection any woman can have . . . is courage."

—ELIZABETH CADY STANTON

10-MINUTE LIFE CHANGERS

Squeeze in these mini but mighty challenges to speed your results and feel great.

SET YOURSELF UP FOR SUCCESS : Write down your three biggest goals for today.

1 _____

2 _____

3 _____

10-MINUTE RECHARGE

What _____ 🕑 _____

10-MINUTE MINDFUL MEAL

What _____ 🕑 _____

10-MINUTE WALK

Where _____ 🕑 _____

10-MINUTE TECH BREAK

What _____ 🕑 _____

NOTES: _____

_____

fit in 10 TONING TRACKER

☐ Yes, I did my Fit in 10 workout!

TODAY'S WORKOUT: Lean and Lovely Legs

WORKOUT NOTES: How did you feel today? What progress are you making when it comes to your strength and fitness goals? Jot it down here.

_____

_____

_____

fit in 10 FOOD TRACKER

BREAKFAST: _____

SNACK: _____

LUNCH: _____

DINNER: _____

SNACK: _____

fit in 10 WATER TRACKER

Aim to drink ten 8-ounce glasses of H_2O each day. Cross them off as you go!

fit in 10 MOOD TRACKER

How are you feeling today? Circle any that apply and make notes below.

HAPPY   PROUD   FOCUSED   ENERGIZED   STRONG   SAD   TIRED   FRUSTRATED

NOTES: _____

_____

_____

{ **DATE:** }

"Our bodies are our gardens, to which our wills are gardeners."

—WILLIAM SHAKESPEARE

I⊘-MINUTE LIFE CHANGERS

Squeeze in these mini but mighty challenges to speed your results and feel great.

SET YOURSELF UP FOR SUCCESS: Write down your three biggest goals for today.

1 _____

2 _____

3 _____

I0-MINUTE RECHARGE

What _____ 🕑 _____

I0-MINUTE MINDFUL MEAL

What _____ 🕑 _____

I0-MINUTE WALK

Where _____ 🕑 _____

I0-MINUTE TECH BREAK

What _____ 🕑 _____

NOTES: _____

_____

fit in 10 TONING TRACKER _____

☐ Yes, I did my Fit in 10 workout!

TODAY'S WORKOUT: Dare to Bare Arms + Tummy Love

WORKOUT NOTES: How did you feel today? What progress are you making when it comes to your strength and fitness goals? Jot it down here.

_____

_____

fit in 10 FOOD TRACKER _____

BREAKFAST: _____

SNACK: _____

LUNCH: _____

DINNER: _____

SNACK: _____

fit in 10 WATER TRACKER _____

Aim to drink ten 8-ounce glasses of H$_2$O each day. Cross them off as you go!

🥛 🥛 🥛 🥛 🥛 🥛 🥛 🥛 🥛 🥛

fit in 10 MOOD TRACKER _____

How are you feeling today? Circle any that apply and make notes below.

😄 HAPPY   🙂 PROUD   🤓 FOCUSED   😎 ENERGIZED   😊 STRONG   😢 SAD   😮 TIRED   😖 FRUSTRATED

NOTES: _____

_____

_____

{ DATE: }

*"It is better to offer no excuse
than a bad one."*

—GEORGE WASHINGTON

———— 1Ⓒ-MINUTE LIFE CHANGERS ————

Squeeze in these mini but mighty challenges to speed your results and feel great.

SET YOURSELF UP FOR SUCCESS : Write down your three biggest goals for today.

1 _____

2 _____

3 _____

10-MINUTE RECHARGE

What _____ 🕑 _____

10-MINUTE MINDFUL MEAL

What _____ 🕑 _____

10-MINUTE WALK

Where _____ 🕑 _____

10-MINUTE TECH BREAK

What _____ 🕑 _____

NOTES: _____

_____

fit in 10 TONING TRACKER _____ ☐ Yes, I did my Fit in 10 workout!

TODAY'S WORKOUT: Torch to Tone

WORKOUT NOTES: How did you feel today? What progress are you making when it comes to your strength and fitness goals? Jot it down here.

_____

_____

fit in 10 FOOD TRACKER _____

BREAKFAST: _____

SNACK: _____

LUNCH: _____

DINNER: _____

SNACK: _____

fit in 10 WATER TRACKER _____

Aim to drink ten 8-ounce glasses of H_2O each day. Cross them off as you go!

fit in 10 MOOD TRACKER _____

How are you feeling today? Circle any that apply and make notes below.

| HAPPY | PROUD | FOCUSED | ENERGIZED | STRONG | SAD | TIRED | FRUSTRATED |

NOTES: _____

_____

_____

{ DATE: }

*"The most difficult thing is the decision to act.
The rest is merely tenacity."*

—AMELIA EARHART

1⊘-MINUTE LIFE CHANGERS

Squeeze in these mini but mighty challenges to speed your results and feel great.

SET YOURSELF UP FOR SUCCESS : Write down your three biggest goals for today.

1 _____

2 _____

3 _____

10-MINUTE RECHARGE

What _____ ⊘ _____

10-MINUTE MINDFUL MEAL

What _____ ⊘ _____

10-MINUTE WALK

Where _____ ⊘ _____

10-MINUTE TECH BREAK

What _____ ⊘ _____

NOTES: _____

_____

fit in 10 TONING TRACKER

☐ Yes, I did my Fit in 10 workout!

TODAY'S WORKOUT: Totally Toned Triceps + Flat and Firm Abs

WORKOUT NOTES: How did you feel today? What progress are you making when it comes to your strength and fitness goals? Jot it down here.

_____

_____

fit in 10 FOOD TRACKER

BREAKFAST: _____

SNACK: _____

LUNCH: _____

DINNER: _____

SNACK: _____

fit in 10 WATER TRACKER

Aim to drink ten 8-ounce glasses of H_2O each day. Cross them off as you go!

fit in 10 MOOD TRACKER

How are you feeling today? Circle any that apply and make notes below.

HAPPY   PROUD   FOCUSED   ENERGIZED   STRONG   SAD   TIRED   FRUSTRATED

NOTES: _____

_____

_____

{ DATE: }

"Success is the sum of small efforts, repeated day in and day out."

—ROBERT J. COLLIER

1☉-MINUTE LIFE CHANGERS

Squeeze in these mini but mighty challenges to speed your results and feel great.

SET YOURSELF UP FOR SUCCESS: Write down your three biggest goals for today.

1 _____

2 _____

3 _____

10-MINUTE RECHARGE

What _____ 🕑 _____

10-MINUTE MINDFUL MEAL

What _____ 🕑 _____

10-MINUTE WALK

Where _____ 🕑 _____

10-MINUTE TECH BREAK

What _____ 🕑 _____

NOTES: _____

_____

fit in 10 TONING TRACKER

☐ Yes, I did my Fit in 10 workout!

TODAY'S WORKOUT: Ultimate Booty Lifter

WORKOUT NOTES: How did you feel today? What progress are you making when it comes to your strength and fitness goals? Jot it down here.

fit in 10 FOOD TRACKER

BREAKFAST:

SNACK:

LUNCH:

DINNER:

SNACK:

fit in 10 WATER TRACKER

Aim to drink ten 8-ounce glasses of H_2O each day. Cross them off as you go!

fit in 10 MOOD TRACKER

How are you feeling today? Circle any that apply and make notes below.

HAPPY   PROUD   FOCUSED   ENERGIZED   STRONG   SAD   TIRED   FRUSTRATED

NOTES:

{ DATE: }

"Start by doing what's necessary; then do what's possible; and suddenly you are doing the impossible."

—FRANCIS OF ASSISI

10-MINUTE LIFE CHANGERS

Squeeze in these mini but mighty challenges to speed your results and feel great.

SET YOURSELF UP FOR SUCCESS: Write down your three biggest goals for today.

1 _____

2 _____

3 _____

10-MINUTE RECHARGE

What _____ 🕑 _____

10-MINUTE MINDFUL MEAL

What _____ 🕑 _____

10-MINUTE WALK

Where _____ 🕑 _____

10-MINUTE TECH BREAK

What _____ 🕑 _____

NOTES: _____

_____

fit in 10 TONING TRACKER

☐ Yes, I did my Fit in 10 workout!

TODAY'S WORKOUT: Sizzle and Sculpt

WORKOUT NOTES: How did you feel today? What progress are you making when it comes to your strength and fitness goals? Jot it down here.

_____

_____

fit in 10 FOOD TRACKER

BREAKFAST: _____

SNACK: _____

LUNCH: _____

DINNER: _____

SNACK: _____

fit in 10 WATER TRACKER

Aim to drink ten 8-ounce glasses of H_2O each day. Cross them off as you go!

fit in 10 MOOD TRACKER

How are you feeling today? Circle any that apply and make notes below.

HAPPY   PROUD   FOCUSED   ENERGIZED   STRONG   SAD   TIRED   FRUSTRATED

NOTES: _____

_____

{ DATE: }

"The world of achievement has always belonged to the optimist."

—J. HAROLD WILKINS

─────── ## 10-MINUTE LIFE CHANGERS ───────

Squeeze in these mini but mighty challenges to speed your results and feel great.

SET YOURSELF UP FOR SUCCESS: Write down your three biggest goals for today.

1 _____

2 _____

3 _____

10-MINUTE RECHARGE

What _____ 🕐 _____

10-MINUTE MINDFUL MEAL

What _____ 🕐 _____

10-MINUTE WALK

Where _____ 🕐 _____

10-MINUTE TECH BREAK

What _____ 🕐 _____

NOTES: _____

_____

fit TONING TRACKER _____ ☐ Yes, I did my Fit in 10 workout!

TODAY'S WORKOUT: Lean and Lovely Legs + Back to Strong*

WORKOUT NOTES: How did you feel today? What progress are you making when it comes to your strength and fitness goals? Jot it down here.

_____

_____

fit FOOD TRACKER _____

BREAKFAST: _____

SNACK: _____

LUNCH: _____

DINNER: _____

SNACK: _____

fit WATER TRACKER _____

Aim to drink ten 8-ounce glasses of H_2O each day. Cross them off as you go!

▢ ▢ ▢ ▢ ▢ ▢ ▢ ▢ ▢ ▢

fit MOOD TRACKER _____

How are you feeling today? Circle any that apply and make notes below.

😄 😊 🤓 😣 😁 🙁 😮 😖
HAPPY PROUD FOCUSED ENERGIZED STRONG SAD TIRED FRUSTRATED

NOTES: _____

_____

*optional

117

{ DATE: }

"Most folks are about as happy as they make up their minds to be."

—ABRAHAM LINCOLN

10-MINUTE LIFE CHANGERS

Squeeze in these mini but mighty challenges to speed your results and feel great.

SET YOURSELF UP FOR SUCCESS: Write down your three biggest goals for today.

1 _____

2 _____

3 _____

10-MINUTE RECHARGE

What _____ 🕐 _____

10-MINUTE MINDFUL MEAL

What _____ 🕐 _____

10-MINUTE WALK

Where _____ 🕐 _____

10-MINUTE TECH BREAK

What _____ 🕐 _____

NOTES: _____

_____

 **TONING TRACKER** ⸻ ☐ Yes, I did my Fit in 10 workout!

TODAY'S WORKOUT: Flat and Firm Abs

WORKOUT NOTES: How did you feel today? What progress are you making when it comes to your strength and fitness goals? Jot it down here.

_____

_____

fit IN 10 **FOOD TRACKER** ⸻

BREAKFAST: _____

SNACK: _____

LUNCH: _____

DINNER: _____

SNACK: _____

fit IN 10 **WATER TRACKER** ⸻

Aim to drink ten 8-ounce glasses of H$_2$O each day. Cross them off as you go!

🥛 🥛 🥛 🥛 🥛 🥛 🥛 🥛 🥛 🥛

fit IN 10 **MOOD TRACKER** ⸻

How are you feeling today? Circle any that apply and make notes below.

HAPPY   PROUD   FOCUSED   ENERGIZED   STRONG   SAD   TIRED   FRUSTRATED

NOTES: _____

_____

{ DATE: }

"An obstacle is often a stepping-stone."

—WILLIAM PRESCOTT

1⊘-MINUTE LIFE CHANGERS

Squeeze in these mini but mighty challenges to speed your results and feel great.

SET YOURSELF UP FOR SUCCESS: Write down your three biggest goals for today.

1 _____

2 _____

3 _____

I0-MINUTE RECHARGE

What _____ 🕐 _____

I0-MINUTE MINDFUL MEAL

What _____ 🕐 _____

I0-MINUTE WALK

Where _____ 🕐 _____

I0-MINUTE TECH BREAK

What _____ 🕐 _____

NOTES: _____

_____

fit IN 10 TONING TRACKER _____ ☐ Yes, I did my Fit in 10 workout!

TODAY'S WORKOUT: Meta Blast

WORKOUT NOTES: How did you feel today? What progress are you making when it comes to your strength and fitness goals? Jot it down here.

_____

_____

fit IN 10 FOOD TRACKER _____

BREAKFAST: _____

SNACK: _____

LUNCH: _____

DINNER: _____

SNACK: _____

fit IN 10 WATER TRACKER _____

Aim to drink ten 8-ounce glasses of H_2O each day. Cross them off as you go!

fit IN 10 MOOD TRACKER _____

How are you feeling today? Circle any that apply and make notes below.

| HAPPY | PROUD | FOCUSED | ENERGIZED | STRONG | SAD | TIRED | FRUSTRATED |

NOTES: _____

_____

_____

Cycle 6

DAYS 51–60

"Just when the caterpillar thought the world was over . . . it became a butterfly."

—ENGLISH PROVERB

Welcome to cycle 6, your final cycle of the Fit in 10 Plan! Hopefully by now you've discovered how easy it can be to eat clean, lose weight, and tone your body in just 10 minutes a day.

What changes have you noticed in your energy levels and body? Have family and friends started to comment on your transformation? Are you excited about buying some new clothes, or feeling more confident about an upcoming event? Whatever it is, make sure to celebrate the strides you've made towards good health and a toned body—and sticking with the program.

Now it's time to keep the transformation going. For the next 10 days, you're going to push yourself with the Fit in 10 routines (yep, they'll get a little harder this round to make sure you continue to see results) and stick with your clean eating. Remember to write down your meals in order to continue building lean muscle and burning fat.

We'll also add one more 10-Minute Life Changer to your daily goals. Stick with it, and you'll feel stronger, leaner, and happier. Let's get ready to end strong!

10-MINUTE LIFE CHANGER
Talk to a Friend

In this tech-savvy world, sometimes it's easy to forget to do something as simple as having a real, face-to-face conversation with a family member or friend. Instead, many of us spend more time texting or messaging—and research shows that a lack of regular human connection can negatively impact our happiness. A Greek study published in the *Journal of Psychosocial Research on Cyberspace* found that people who spend more time on social media are more likely to be depressed.

So, for this 10-minute challenge, we simply want you to chat with a friend or loved one, either by phone call or face-to-face. Just make sure that when you are talking, you shut off the tablet, computer, and TV. You'll be sure to get an instant happiness boost!

{ DATE: }

*"Find a group of people who challenge
and inspire you, spend a lot of time with them,
and it will change your life."*

—AMY POEHLER

1⊙-MINUTE LIFE CHANGERS

Squeeze in these mini but mighty challenges to speed your results and feel great.

SET YOURSELF UP FOR SUCCESS: Write down your three biggest goals for today.

1 _____

2 _____

3 _____

1O-MINUTE RECHARGE

What _____ 🕐 _____

1O-MINUTE MINDFUL MEAL

What _____ 🕐 _____

1O-MINUTE WALK

Where _____ 🕐 _____

1O-MINUTE TECH BREAK

What _____ 🕐 _____

1O-MINUTE TALK

Who _____ 🕐 _____

fit in 10 TONING TRACKER

☐ Yes, I did my Fit in 10 workout!

TODAY'S WORKOUT: Ultimate Booty Lifter + Tummy Love*

WORKOUT NOTES: How did you feel today? What progress are you making when it comes to your strength and fitness goals? Jot it down here.

_____

_____

fit in 10 FOOD TRACKER

BREAKFAST: _____

SNACK: _____

LUNCH: _____

DINNER: _____

SNACK: _____

fit in 10 WATER TRACKER

Aim to drink ten 8-ounce glasses of H_2O each day. Cross them off as you go!

fit in 10 MOOD TRACKER

How are you feeling today? Circle any that apply and make notes below.

| HAPPY | PROUD | FOCUSED | ENERGIZED | STRONG | SAD | TIRED | FRUSTRATED |

NOTES: _____

_____

*optional

{ DATE: }

*"Talking about our problems is our greatest addiction.
Break the habit. Talk about your joys."*

—RITA SCHIANO

1Ⓞ-MINUTE LIFE CHANGERS

Squeeze in these mini but mighty challenges to speed your results and feel great.

SET YOURSELF UP FOR SUCCESS: Write down your three biggest goals for today.

1 _____

2 _____

3 _____

10-MINUTE RECHARGE

What _____ 🕐 _____

10-MINUTE MINDFUL MEAL

What _____ 🕐 _____

10-MINUTE WALK

Where _____ 🕐 _____

10-MINUTE TECH BREAK

What _____ 🕐 _____

10-MINUTE TALK

Who _____ 🕐 _____

fit
IN 10 TONING TRACKER _____ ☐ Yes, I did my Fit in 10 workout!

TODAY'S WORKOUT: *Sizzle and Sculpt*

WORKOUT NOTES: How did you feel today? What progress are you making when it comes to your strength and fitness goals? Jot it down here.

_____

_____

fit
IN 10 FOOD TRACKER _____

BREAKFAST: _____

SNACK: _____

LUNCH: _____

DINNER: _____

SNACK: _____

fit
IN 10 WATER TRACKER _____

Aim to drink ten 8-ounce glasses of H_2O each day. Cross them off as you go!

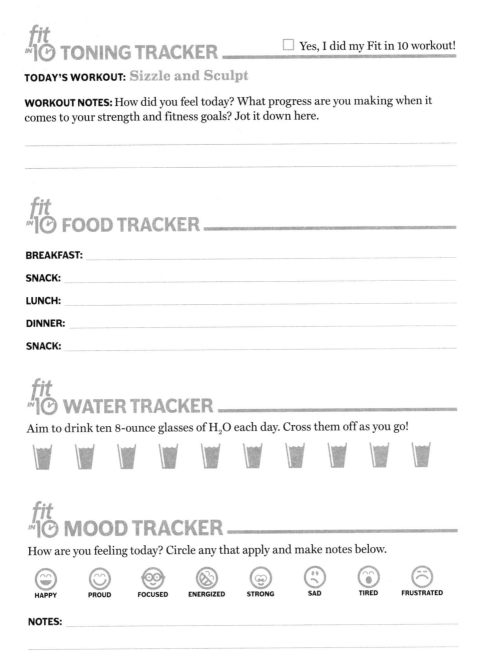

fit
IN 10 MOOD TRACKER _____

How are you feeling today? Circle any that apply and make notes below.

HAPPY   PROUD   FOCUSED   ENERGIZED   STRONG   SAD   TIRED   FRUSTRATED

NOTES: _____

_____

_____

{ DATE: }

"Do not fear going forward slowly;
fear only to stand still."

—CHINESE PROVERB

1○-MINUTE LIFE CHANGERS

Squeeze in these mini but mighty challenges to speed your results and feel great.

SET YOURSELF UP FOR SUCCESS: Write down your three biggest goals for today.

1 _____
2 _____
3 _____

I0-MINUTE RECHARGE

What _____ 🕑 _____

I0-MINUTE MINDFUL MEAL

What _____ 🕑 _____

I0-MINUTE WALK

Where _____ 🕑 _____

I0-MINUTE TECH BREAK

What _____ 🕑 _____

I0-MINUTE TALK

Who _____ 🕑 _____

fit in 10 TONING TRACKER

TODAY'S WORKOUT: Lean and Lovely Legs + Back to Strong*

WORKOUT NOTES: How did you feel today? What progress are you making when it comes to your strength and fitness goals? Jot it down here.

_____

_____

fit in 10 FOOD TRACKER

BREAKFAST: _____

SNACK: _____

LUNCH: _____

DINNER: _____

SNACK: _____

fit in 10 WATER TRACKER

Aim to drink ten 8-ounce glasses of H_2O each day. Cross them off as you go!

fit in 10 MOOD TRACKER

How are you feeling today? Circle any that apply and make notes below.

| HAPPY | PROUD | FOCUSED | ENERGIZED | STRONG | SAD | TIRED | FRUSTRATED |

NOTES: _____

_____

_____

*optional

{ DATE: }

*"The mind is everything.
What you think you become."*

—BUDDHA

1⊙-MINUTE LIFE CHANGERS

Squeeze in these mini but mighty challenges to speed your results and feel great.

SET YOURSELF UP FOR SUCCESS: Write down your three biggest goals for today.

1 _____

2 _____

3 _____

10-MINUTE RECHARGE

What _____ 🕐 _____

10-MINUTE MINDFUL MEAL

What _____ 🕐 _____

10-MINUTE WALK

Where _____ 🕐 _____

10-MINUTE TECH BREAK

What _____ 🕐 _____

10-MINUTE TALK

Who _____ 🕐 _____

fit in 10 TONING TRACKER

☐ Yes, I did my Fit in 10 workout!

TODAY'S WORKOUT: Dare to Bare Arms

WORKOUT NOTES: How did you feel today? What progress are you making when it comes to your strength and fitness goals? Jot it down here.

_____

_____

fit in 10 FOOD TRACKER

BREAKFAST: _____

SNACK: _____

LUNCH: _____

DINNER: _____

SNACK: _____

fit in 10 WATER TRACKER

Aim to drink ten 8-ounce glasses of H$_2$O each day. Cross them off as you go!

fit in 10 MOOD TRACKER

How are you feeling today? Circle any that apply and make notes below.

HAPPY   PROUD   FOCUSED   ENERGIZED   STRONG   SAD   TIRED   FRUSTRATED

NOTES: _____

_____

{ DATE: }

"Fall seven times and stand up eight!"

—JAPANESE PROVERB

—— 10-MINUTE LIFE CHANGERS ——

Squeeze in these mini but mighty challenges to speed your results and feel great.

SET YOURSELF UP FOR SUCCESS: Write down your three biggest goals for today.

1 _____

2 _____

3 _____

10-MINUTE RECHARGE

What _____ 🕐 _____

10-MINUTE MINDFUL MEAL

What _____ 🕐 _____

10-MINUTE WALK

Where _____ 🕐 _____

10-MINUTE TECH BREAK

What _____ 🕐 _____

10-MINUTE TALK

Who _____ 🕐 _____

fit in 10 TONING TRACKER

☐ Yes, I did my Fit in 10 workout!

TODAY'S WORKOUT: Meta Blast + Deep Core*

WORKOUT NOTES: How did you feel today? What progress are you making when it comes to your strength and fitness goals? Jot it down here.

_____

_____

fit in 10 FOOD TRACKER

BREAKFAST: _____

SNACK: _____

LUNCH: _____

DINNER: _____

SNACK: _____

fit in 10 WATER TRACKER

Aim to drink ten 8-ounce glasses of H$_2$O each day. Cross them off as you go!

🥛 🥛 🥛 🥛 🥛 🥛 🥛 🥛 🥛 🥛

fit in 10 MOOD TRACKER

How are you feeling today? Circle any that apply and make notes below.

HAPPY · PROUD · FOCUSED · ENERGIZED · STRONG · SAD · TIRED · FRUSTRATED

NOTES: _____

_____

*optional

133

{ DATE: }

"Believe and act as if it were impossible to fail."

—CHARLES KETTERING

1⊘-MINUTE LIFE CHANGERS

Squeeze in these mini but mighty challenges to speed your results and feel great.

SET YOURSELF UP FOR SUCCESS: Write down your three biggest goals for today.

1 _____

2 _____

3 _____

1O-MINUTE RECHARGE

What _____ 🕐 _____

1O-MINUTE MINDFUL MEAL

What _____ 🕐 _____

1O-MINUTE WALK

Where _____ 🕐 _____

1O-MINUTE TECH BREAK

What _____ 🕐 _____

1O-MINUTE TALK

Who _____ 🕐 _____

 **TONING TRACKER** ☐ Yes, I did my Fit in 10 workout!

TODAY'S WORKOUT: Happy Hipster

WORKOUT NOTES: How did you feel today? What progress are you making when it comes to your strength and fitness goals? Jot it down here.

 **FOOD TRACKER**

BREAKFAST:

SNACK:

LUNCH:

DINNER:

SNACK:

WATER TRACKER

Aim to drink ten 8-ounce glasses of H_2O each day. Cross them off as you go!

MOOD TRACKER

How are you feeling today? Circle any that apply and make notes below.

HAPPY PROUD FOCUSED ENERGIZED STRONG SAD TIRED FRUSTRATED

NOTES:

{ DATE: }

*"Only put off until tomorrow what you are
willing to die having left undone."*

—PABLO PICASSO

─────── **10-MINUTE LIFE CHANGERS** ───────

Squeeze in these mini but mighty challenges to speed your results and feel great.

SET YOURSELF UP FOR SUCCESS: Write down your three biggest goals for today.

1 _____

2 _____

3 _____

10-MINUTE RECHARGE

What _____ 🕐 _____

10-MINUTE MINDFUL MEAL

What _____ 🕐 _____

10-MINUTE WALK

Where _____ 🕐 _____

10-MINUTE TECH BREAK

What _____ 🕐 _____

10-MINUTE TALK

Who _____ 🕐 _____

fit IN 10 TONING TRACKER

☐ Yes, I did my Fit in 10 workout!

TODAY'S WORKOUT: Torch to Tone

WORKOUT NOTES: How did you feel today? What progress are you making when it comes to your strength and fitness goals? Jot it down here.

_____

_____

fit IN 10 FOOD TRACKER

BREAKFAST: _____

SNACK: _____

LUNCH: _____

DINNER: _____

SNACK: _____

fit IN 10 WATER TRACKER

Aim to drink ten 8-ounce glasses of H_2O each day. Cross them off as you go!

fit IN 10 MOOD TRACKER

How are you feeling today? Circle any that apply and make notes below.

HAPPY PROUD FOCUSED ENERGIZED STRONG SAD TIRED FRUSTRATED

NOTES: _____

_____

_____

{ DATE: }

*"Not knowing when the dawn will come,
I open every door."*

—EMILY DICKINSON

10-MINUTE LIFE CHANGERS

Squeeze in these mini but mighty challenges to speed your results and feel great.

SET YOURSELF UP FOR SUCCESS: Write down your three biggest goals for today.

1 _____

2 _____

3 _____

10-MINUTE RECHARGE

What _____ 🕐 _____

10-MINUTE MINDFUL MEAL

What _____ 🕐 _____

10-MINUTE WALK

Where _____ 🕐 _____

10-MINUTE TECH BREAK

What _____ 🕐 _____

10-MINUTE TALK

Who _____ 🕐 _____

fit TONING TRACKER _____ ☐ Yes, I did my Fit in 10 workout!

TODAY'S WORKOUT: Ultimate Booty Lifter + Totally Toned Triceps*

WORKOUT NOTES: How did you feel today? What progress are you making when it comes to your strength and fitness goals? Jot it down here.

_____

_____

fit FOOD TRACKER _____

BREAKFAST: _____

SNACK: _____

LUNCH: _____

DINNER: _____

SNACK: _____

fit WATER TRACKER _____

Aim to drink ten 8-ounce glasses of H_2O each day. Cross them off as you go!

fit MOOD TRACKER _____

How are you feeling today? Circle any that apply and make notes below.

HAPPY PROUD FOCUSED ENERGIZED STRONG SAD TIRED FRUSTRATED

NOTES: _____

_____

_____

*optional

{ DATE: }

*"I attribute my success to this.
I never gave or took an excuse."*

—FLORENCE NIGHTINGALE

10-MINUTE LIFE CHANGERS

Squeeze in these mini but mighty challenges to speed your results and feel great.

SET YOURSELF UP FOR SUCCESS : Write down your three biggest goals for today.

1 _____

2 _____

3 _____

10-MINUTE RECHARGE

What _____ 🕐 _____

10-MINUTE MINDFUL MEAL

What _____ 🕐 _____

10-MINUTE WALK

Where _____ 🕐 _____

10-MINUTE TECH BREAK

What _____ 🕐 _____

10-MINUTE TALK

Who _____ 🕐 _____

fit IN 10 TONING TRACKER

☐ Yes, I did my Fit in 10 workout!

TODAY'S WORKOUT: Flat and Firm Abs + Lean and Lovely Legs

WORKOUT NOTES: How did you feel today? What progress are you making when it comes to your strength and fitness goals? Jot it down here.

fit IN 10 FOOD TRACKER

BREAKFAST:

SNACK:

LUNCH:

DINNER:

SNACK:

fit IN 10 WATER TRACKER

Aim to drink ten 8-ounce glasses of H_2O each day. Cross them off as you go!

fit IN 10 MOOD TRACKER

How are you feeling today? Circle any that apply and make notes below.

HAPPY PROUD FOCUSED ENERGIZED STRONG SAD TIRED FRUSTRATED

NOTES:

{ DATE: }

*"In the end, it's not the years in your
life that count. It's the life in your years."*

—ABRAHAM LINCOLN

1⊘-MINUTE LIFE CHANGERS

Squeeze in these mini but mighty challenges to speed your results and feel great.

SET YOURSELF UP FOR SUCCESS : Write down your three biggest goals for today.

1 _____
2 _____
3 _____

10-MINUTE RECHARGE

What _____ 🕐 ____

10-MINUTE MINDFUL MEAL

What _____ 🕐 ____

10-MINUTE WALK

Where _____ 🕐 ____

10-MINUTE TECH BREAK

What _____ 🕐 ____

10-MINUTE TALK

Who _____ 🕐 ____

fit IN 10 TONING TRACKER

☐ Yes, I did my Fit in 10 workout!

TODAY'S WORKOUT: Sizzle and Sculpt

WORKOUT NOTES: How did you feel today? What progress are you making when it comes to your strength and fitness goals? Jot it down here.

_____

_____

fit IN 10 FOOD TRACKER

BREAKFAST: _____

SNACK: _____

LUNCH: _____

DINNER: _____

SNACK: _____

fit IN 10 WATER TRACKER

Aim to drink ten 8-ounce glasses of H_2O each day. Cross them off as you go!

fit IN 10 MOOD TRACKER

How are you feeling today? Circle any that apply and make notes below.

HAPPY   PROUD   FOCUSED   ENERGIZED   STRONG   SAD   TIRED   FRUSTRATED

NOTES: _____

_____

_____